In the Name of God, the Beneficent the Merciful.

Copyright © 2024 by Zahra Mansouri

All rights reserved. No part of this publication may be reproduced, distributed, or transmitted in any form or by any means, including photocopying, recording, or other electronic or mechanical methods, without the prior written permission of the publisher, except in the case of brief quotations embodied in critical reviews and certain other noncommercial uses permitted by copyright law. For permission requests, write to the publisher, addressed "Attention: - Permissions (The Day of Ashura)," at the email address below.

Lantern Publications
info@lanternpublications.com
www.lanternkids.com.au

Ordering Information:
Quantity sales. Special discounts are available on quantity purchases by corporations, associations, and others. For details, contact the distributor at the address above.

Written by: Zahra Mansouri | **Illustrated by:** Zille Abbas

ISBN- 978-1-922583-68-0
Abbreviations used in this book:
(as)- Alayhis Salaam – May peace be upon him.

Second Edition

 A catalogue record for this book is available from the National Library of Australia

AHLULBAIT COMIC BOOKS

WRITTEN BY: ZAHRA MANSOURI
@AHLULBAIT_COMIC_BOOKS

ILLUSTRATED BY: ZILL E ABBAS
@SHADOWOFABBAS

...HAT TOOK PLACE IN KARBALA WAS THE PEAK OF ALL BATTLES BETWEEN THE ...RCES OF GOOD VERSUS THE FORCES OF EVIL. WHILST THIS CLASH HAD BEGUN ...GHT FROM THE TIME OF PROPHET ADAM (A.S), THERE ARE SOME SPECIFIC KEY ...INTS IN HISTORY WHERE THE EVENTS OF ASHURA CAN BE TRACED BACK TO. ONE OF ...E FIRST INSTANCES WAS WHERE POWER HUNGRY INDIVIDUALS COULD NO LONGER ...AR IMAM ALI'S (A.S) UNWAVERING COMMITMENT TO ESTABLISHING JUSTICE.

THIS ENMITY DATES BACK TO 661 AD, WHEN THE RIGHTFUL CALIPH, IMAM ALI (A.S), WAS ASSASSINATED DURING HIS SALAH. IBN MULJIM STRUCK HIM ON THE HEAD WITH HIS SWORD AS THE IMAM WAS IN PROSTRATION.

THE STRIKE ITSELF DID NOT KILL THE IMAM, BUT IT WAS THE POISON THAT IBN MULJIM SOAKED HIS SWORD IN WHICH LEAD TO IMAM ALI'S (A.S) MARTYDOM ON THE NIGHT OF QADR.

AFTER THE PASSING OF IMAM ALI (A.S), HIS ELDER SON, HASSAN AL MUJTABA (A.S) W/ DIVINELY APPOINTED AS THE IMAM OF THE TIME AND SO IT WAS HIS TURN T FOLLOW IN HIS FATHER'S FOOTSTEPS OF ESTABLISHING A SOCIETY BOUND E JUSTICE. HOWEVER, THE ENEMIES OF ISLAM HAD NOT FINISHED YET...

THE MUSLIM UMMAH WAS DIVIDED OVE WHETHER MUAWIYA OR IMAM HASSAN (A: SHOULD BE THE NEXT RULER. THI FUELLED FURTHER CONFLICT UNTI MUAWIYA SEIZED THE POSITION.

MUAWIYA HAD LEFT NO OPTION BUT FO IMAM HASSAN (A.S) TO SIGN A PEAC TREATY. AS PART OF THE DEAL, MUAWIY AGREED NOT TO APPOINT A SUCCESSOR T(THE CALIPHATE. BUT THIS WAS JUST PLOT TO SHOW THE PEOPLE HOW TH IMAM HAS AGREED WITH HIS RULERSHIP...

WAS NOT LONG BEFORE THE CHARACTER AND INFLUENCE OF IMAM HASSAN (A.S)
SO BECAME UNBEARABLE TO WHICH, HE TOO, WAS MARTYRED. IN 670AD, HIS OWN
FE, BINT AL ASH'ATH HAD POISONED HIM IN RETURN FOR PROMISED POWER!

ITH NO MORE FRICTION FROM IMAM HASSAN (A.S), MUAWIYA SEIZED THE
PORTUNITY TO BREAK THE TREATY AND DECLARES THAT HE HAS APPOINTED HIS
N YAZID TO BE THE CALIPH AFTER HIM.

FEW YEARS LATER AND MUAWIYA DIES OF AN ILLNESS. YAZID TAKES OVER, BEGINS
O SPREAD CORRUPTION AND VIOLENCE THROUGH HIS SOLDIERS. BUT AT THE SAME
IME DEMANDING ALLEGIANCE FROM ALL MUSLIMS!

YAZID KNEW THAT IF HE WANTED TO AUTHORIZE HIS RULE AND MAKE IT SEE LEGITIMATE, THEN HE WOULD HAVE TO RECEIVE IMAM HUSSAIN'S (A.S) PLEDGE C ALLEGIANCE. BUT WHEN INVITING HIM TO DO SO, THE IMAM NOT ONLY REFUSED, BL HE MADE CLEAR THAT HE STOOD FOR JUSTICE AND TRUTH, NOT TYRANNY.

"I AM READY TO FIGHT FOR THE SOLE GOAL OF SEEKING REFORM OF THE UMMAH OF MY GRANDFATHER, THE PROPHET OF ALLAH! I WANT TO ENJOIN GOOD AND FORBID EVIL."

BECAUSE OF THIS, IMAM HUSSAIN (A.S) WAS FORCED TO FLEE MEDINA UNDER TH THREAT OF IMPRISONMENT AND ASSASSINATION BY YAZID. HE SET OFF TO KUF IRAQ, WITH HIS FAMILY AND FOLLOWERS AFTER RECEIVING TWELVE THOUSAN LETTERS FROM THE PEOPLE OF KUFA PLEDGING SUPPORT FOR AN UPRISIN AGAINST YAZID.

BEFORE IMAM HUSSAIN (A.S REACHED KUFA, HE WENT TO MAKKA TO PERFORM HAJJ. HOWEVER, BEFC RE COMPLETING THE PILGRIMAG HE DEPARTED FOR KUFA IN ORDE TO AVOID THE THREAT OF FURTHE VIOLENCE AND TO PRESERVE TH SANCTITY OF THE HOLY CITY.

THE MEANTIME YAZID SENT A GOVERNOR TO KUFA, THREATENING THE PEOPLE WITH VIOLENCE IF THEY DID NOT ABANDON THEIR SUPPORT FOR THE UPRISING WITH IMAM HUSSAIN (A.S). THIS CAUSED THOUSANDS OF KUFANS TO WITHDRAW THEIR SUPPORT FOR THE HOLY IMAM.

REWARDS WILL BE GIVEN FOR ALL WHO BETRAY HUSSAIN!

ON THE WAY TO KUFA, IMAM HUSSAIN (A.S) AND HIS GROUP WERE INTERCEPTED BY YAZID'S ARMY, LED BY A MAN NAMED HURR AL-RIYAHI (A.S), AND FORCED TO CAMP IN THE DESERT OF KARBALA.

YAZID'S FORCES THEN QUICKLY ENCIRCLED IMAM HUSSAIN'S (A.S) CAMP AND CUT OFF ACCESS TO THE EUPHRATES RIVER (AL FURAT), DEPRIVING THEM OF WATER. THEY LEFT THE MEN, WOMEN, AND CHILDREN TO SUFFER FROM 3 DAYS OF UNBEARABLE THIRST IN IRAQ"S HOT DESERT HEAT.

THE NIGHT BEFORE ASHURA, IMAM HUSSAIN (A.S) GATHERED HIS COMPANIONS AND OFFERED THEM THE CHANCE TO LEAVE WITHOUT JUDGING THEM, BUT THEY ALL CHOSE TO STAY AND SUPPORT THE IMAM OF THEIR TIME.

ON THE MORNING OF ASHURA, IMA HUSSAIN (A.S) DELIVERED A POWERFU SPEECH, REMINDING HIS ENEMIES THA HE WAS STILL THE GRANDSON OF T PROPHET AND THAT HE WISHED TO LEAV PEACEFULLY.

MOVED BY HIS HEART WRENCHING SPEECH, HURR AL-RIYAHHI (A.S) AND A FEW MORE FROM YAZID"S ARMY ABANDONED YAZID TO JOIN THE IMAM'S ETERNAL STAND FOR JUSTICE.

EVEN THOUGH YAZEED ENJOYE STARTING THE BATTLE KNOWING H HAD 30,000 SOLDIERS, THE 7 COMPANIONS DID NOT BLINK AN EY DUE TO THEIR FAITH IN THE IMAM.

THE COMPANIONS DID NO ALLOW IMAM HUSSAIN" (A.S) FAMILY TO GO INT THE BATTLEFIELD BEFOR THEM.

SO EACH OF THEM TOO TURNS RACING INTO TH BATTLEFIELD, FIGHTIN AS HARD AS THEY COUL UNTIL THEY EVENTUALL BECAME MARTYRS...

IMAM HASSAN'S (A.S) 13-YEAR-OLD SON, AL-QASIM, HEARD HIS UNCLE IMAM HUSSAIN (A.S) CALLING FOR PEOPLE TO JOIN THE BATTLE AGAINST TYRANNY. SO HE PRESENTED THE LETTER OF HIS FATHER PROVING HIS PERMISSION TO FIGHT WHERE HE TOO WAS MARTYRED. SOON AFTER, IMAM HUSSAIN 'S 18 YEAR OLD SON ALI AKBAR (A.S) ALSO FOUGHT VALIANTLY AND WAS MARTYRED. NOW THE IMAM WAS TRULY ALONE!

THE CRIES OF THE CHILDREN WERE GETTING LOUDER FROM THEIR THIRST SO THE IMAM RAISED HIS 6 MONTH OLD BABY ALI ASGHAR (A.S) PLEADING FOR WATER TO WHICH A FATAL ARROW WAS SHOT AT HIS NECK. HE BECAME THE YOUNGEST MARTYR.

WHILE IMAM HUSSAIN (A.S) AND HIS SOLDIERS WERE IN BATTLE, HIS DAUGHTER SAKINA (A.S) AND THE OTHER CHILDREN ASKED ABAL FAZL ABBAS (A.S) TO FETCH WATER FROM THE RIVER, AS THEY HAD BEEN WITHOUT WATER AND FOOD FOR 3 DAYS.

ABBAS (A.S) WENT TO THE RIVER TO GET WATER FOR THE THIRSTY CHILDREN. HE FILLED HIS BAG BUT REFRAINED FROM DRINKING ANY HIMSELF, AS HE WAS DEVOTED TO IMAM HUSSAIN (A.S) AND COULD NOT BEAR THE THOUGHT OF SAKINA (A.S) AND THE OTHERS BEING THIRSTY. BUT THE TYRANTS WERE WAITING FOR HIM...

ON HIS WAY BACK TO THE CAMP, ABBAS (A.S) WAS ATTACKED BY YAZID'S ARMY. THEY SEVERED BOTH HIS ARMS, SO HE CARRIED THE WATER BAG WITH HIS MOUTH, HOPING TO DELIVER IT TO THE CHILDREN. THEY SHOT HIM WITH ARROWS, AND STRUCK HIM UNTIL HE FELL OFF HIS HORSE AND WAS MARTYRED.

O' MY BROTHER HUSSAIN! YA AKHI HUSSAIN!

With no one left to help him, Imam Hussain (A.S) was left alone and to fight the army of Yazeed in Karbala. He fought valiantly until he was surrounded by enemies and struck off his horse. When surrounded, Shimr approached him and beheaded the Imam in a horrific manner.

The enemy forces attacked and plundered the possessions of the dead bodies as well as the camp of Imam Hussain's family (A.S). The tents were set on fire with the women and children inside, including the granddaughters of the Holy Prophet (PBUH).

THE SURVIVING FAMILY MEMBERS AND SUPPORTERS WERE TAKEN CAPTIVE BY YAZID'S ARMY AND PARADED ALL THE WAY TO DAMASCUS, SYRIA. IT WAS THERE THAT THE MESSAGE OF KARBALA WAS FIERCELY KEPT ALIVE BY IMAM HUSSAIN'S SISTER SYEDA ZAINAB AND HIS SON, THE NEXT IMAM, ZAIN UL ABIDEEN (A.S).

NOW, AS A RESULT OF THEIR PATIENCE AND STRUGGLE TO HONOUR THE SACRIFICE OF THE MARTYRS OF KARBALA, ASHURA IS COMMEMORATED
EVERY YEAR BY SHIA MUSLIMS AROUND THE WORLD TO REMEMBER THE SACRIFICE OF IMAM HUSSAIN (AS) AND HIS COMPANIONS.

L OF THESE EVENTS FOLDED INTO ONE DAY SET A STANDARD FOR US ALL ON HOW
) LIVE. LESSONS FOR EVERY ASPECT OF OUR LIFE CAN BE FOUND IN THE DAY OF
HURA. PEOPLE OF ALL AGES TRY THEIR BEST TO KEEP THIS MESSAGE ALIVE BY
RVING HUMANITY IN ANY WAY POSSIBLE.

E STORY OF ASHURA TEACHES US ABOUT BRAVERY, COMPASSION, LOYALTY AND THE
PORTANCE OF STANDING UP FOR JUSTICE...
JST AS IMAM HUSSAIN (A.S) DID.

"NOW YOU KNOW THE STORY OF ASHURA. LET US ALWAYS REMEMBER TO BE KIND, BRAVE, AND JUST, FOLLOWING THE EXAMPLE OF OUR HOLY IMAM HUSSAIN (AS)."

The day of Ashura, hearts ingrained with sorrow.

Remembering the greatest sacrifices made, a tale of tomorrow.

Rivers made of tears for the martyrs.

Their legacy saving faith, ignite a guiding light.

- Hadieh Rahimi

www.ingramcontent.com/pod-product-compliance
Lightning Source LLC
Chambersburg PA
CBRC090022130526
44590CB00038B/141